There Is a *Blessing* in the Storm

Juanita Witherspoon

ISBN 979-8-88685-223-3 (paperback)
ISBN 979-8-88685-224-0 (digital)

Christian Faith Publishing
832 Park Avenue
Meadville, PA 16335
www.christianfaithpublishing.com

Printed in the United States of America

Acknowledgments

First and most importantly, I have to give the highest thanks to God and his beloved son Jesus Christ who shed his blood and died on the cross so that we could have a chance to be forgiven for the sins that we commit in our lifetime.

I would also like to acknowledge my church family, because even though they didn't know it, but because of their prayers and faith, it helped me through some trying times in my life. To my three daughters, whom I have learned much about myself by watching them grow into adulthood.

To all of my family, I say thank you for your love and support; to my friends who stood by me on the days that the tears would not stop falling, and who are still here as I stand here putting on my best smile. To you, I say thank you.

Last but not least, I would like to say thank you to the man who came into my life and brought back laughter. He got me to see the good things about life again. He made me feel good about myself in a way that I had never experienced in my years of life; I felt like he put me through boot camp; he broke me down only to build me back up again in a positive way. He taught me how to love myself even if no one else did. One thing I learned is that I had to love myself before I could love anyone else. To that, Bo, rest in peace. I just want to say thank you for all that you taught me and for your love.

To my husband James, thanks for your devoted love and support. Love you.

To my friend Derrick, thanks for saving my life and leading me back into the house of God.

To my readers, I just want to entertain you with my creative writing, hoping that you will keep an open mind. Enjoy and continue to support me by reading my novels. Oh yes, there will be more to come, so sit back and enjoy.

Introduction

What if you could go back and change the hands of time? What if you could go back to yesterday instead of being here today? What if there were no racial barriers, wars, or poverty? Would that change who you are today or where you are destined to go? If you knew the things then that you know now, would that help you to become a better person? I think because of past experiences that I have experienced, that has made me become the person that I am today. I would not want to trade places today for yesterday because today is a lot better. I am who I am because of the trials and tribulations of yesterday and today, but tomorrow I will be better.

Well, let me start by introducing myself. I am fifty-seven and still look good. God has really brought me through some storms and I truly thank him. If, may be someone going through something similar, I want you to know God will make a way if you keep the faith and don't give up. I have three beautiful daughters and nine grandchildren and two great grands. I have always enjoyed reading, and it has been a childhood passion to become an author. I always keep a diary of what I want to write about in my head and it's time to get started.

I reside in Washington, DC. My passion has always been to write, but I did not have the means at the time to pursue it. You see, I have been through some rough times in my lifetime. I have been through everything from child abuse, rape, bad marriages, substance abuse and bad relationships—all together. But now, I'm finally starting to get my feet planted with a good-loving man by my side, along with lots of family and friends. Most of all, I have God walking with me holding my hand.

It has taken me all these years to finally open up to the point where I can talk about the things that has happened in my life without feeling ashamed or embarrassed. I am praying that through my experiences, just maybe, it will help someone else who may be experiencing the same thing.

So, I hope that you enjoy reading my story—the situations are true. The character's names are fictitious to protect all the people I love. No matter what I may have gone through, I would not have made it without my faith in God.

Chapter 1

THE BEGINNING

Isaiah 55:6–7, "Seek ye the Lord while he may be found, call ye upon him while he is near. Let the wicked forsake his way and the unrighteous man his thoughts; and let him return unto the Lord, and he will have many upon him; and to our God, for he will abundantly pardon."

This is a story about a quiet, shy and bashful young lady by the name of Chante Lewis. Growing up, she hardly had much to say. Most of the time when you see her, she always had a frown on that pretty face. Whenever people met her for the first time, they would always get the impression that she either hated the world or she was a child full of such heartbreaking sadness.

Chante grew up being raised by her grandfather, Mr. Pearson, and they resided in a part of Washington, DC, that was very popular for its nightlife and numerous bars. There were liquor stores on every corner and churches in between. Chante had been living with her grandfather since she was around six months old.

Let's see if I can recollect.

It all started on a cool fall day, and at this time she was just an infant being cared for by her parents. There were her mother and father—Deidre and Charles—and her three sisters: Alexis, Amanda and Sabrina. On this day, a lot would change for these precious little girls forever. Their lives would be built on lies and deceit. No one

1

would ever guess that they were about to be carried down different paths and in different directions. In their young lives there was about to be some serious changes that only God will be able to help them endure.

Also on that same dreadful day, Deidre will lose her children. They would end up taken from her by the one person that the children were taught to cherish. On that day, it seems like the storm gates of hell opened up when Charles came home to find his babies gone.

Now I know there is a lot of questions going through your head because a lot sure went through mine. I always wondered what really happened on that day? Why were those children taken away from their parents? What happened to the children?

Well, let me see if I can explain.

The three oldest girls were put on a bus bound for Richmond, Virginia. There, they were met by Aunt Agnes, who was their grandfather's sister.

Chapter 2

GRANDDADDY

Psalm 50:14–15, "Offer unto God thanksgiving; and pay thy vows unto the most high: and call upon me in the day of trouble: I will deliver thee, and they shalt glorify me."

Mr. Pearson was the kind of person that found fault in everybody and everything. He simply felt that if he did something for someone, it had to benefit him. *I really don't think that he ever realized that some of the things that he would say about people would reflect on the kind of person he really was.*

During Chante's upbringing years with her grandfather, she will learn that there are many secrets that will unfold. To the outside world, Mr. Pearson appeared to be a caring man who worked very hard. He appeared to live a quiet lifestyle and was very reputable in the neighborhood and his job. But in the privacy of his own home, he was another person all together.

Now don't get me wrong; he was a very educated man but deep down, something kept him angry and bitter especially toward women.

When it came down to his family, sometimes he seemed to love them and then other times he acted like he hated them. While raising Chante, he was very strict and he refused to let her be a child. No matter how many times her mother would plead with her father to let her see her child, he would not budge. If Deidre tried anyway, shape or form to get near Chante, Mr. Pearson would physically chase her away. He would rant and rave as if she was nothing to him.

Mr. Pearson would talk very badly about his daughter to anyone who would listen. He took his raising of Chante very seriously and there was nothing she could do without his consent. He did not like family or friends to just stop by and if they did, he would just stand looking at them out of the peephole in the door.

Chante was only allowed to have friends over very rarely, and that was mostly for her birthday. That's about the only time that he seemed to be okay. She wasn't allowed to go outside and play with other children, and she definitely could not do after-school activities. There was a time limit for her to get from school to home; lucky for her, she lived a couple blocks away.

Now believe it or not, back in those days you got beatings; and Chante got her share of getting her behind tore up, but sometimes they were for silly reasons, like for instance: if she lost her barrettes, being fifteen minutes late from school, or simply playing with dolls that adorned her bed.

Periodically, Chante would get to spend the weekend with her grandmother.

Mrs. Pearson was actually Deidre's stepmother. She was Mr. Pearson's second wife. *I still wonder how he could have left such a beautiful and loving woman.* Mrs. Pearson never made Chante feel unloved. She never made her feel left out or unwanted.

The one thing that she had a passion for was church. It was the one thing that had been introduced to her while living with her grandfather that was good. Most of the tenants in the apartment building that they resided in was mostly elderly, but they really took to Chante. *Sometimes, I think that it was her home life that they pitied. Chante really was a respectful child—she had to be, and she didn't get into a lot of mischief; but then again, could she?*

I don't really think Mr. Pearson knew how to love because if he did, he would have started with learning to love himself; but then, again maybe that was one of the problems—maybe he really did not know how to love himself or anyone else for that matter.

Chapter 3

THE OTHER ONE

Psalms 121:1, "Look to the hills from whence cometh your help, your help cometh from the Lord."

Mr. Pearson did not raise Chante alone, he had some help. He and his mate Brian McFaddon were lovers. Brian started out a really kind and sincere person. He felt his job was to raise Chante to have a good life. He wanted to see her finish school and go off to college. He wanted to be able to walk her down the aisle on her wedding day. Brian truly loved Chante; for the brief time that they had together, she loved him, too.

Unfortunately, none of the things that Brian had planned to see would happen because he passed away when Chante was around seven. Soon after Brian's death, Chante was sent to Arlington, Virginia. to live with an elderly lady and her son for about a year. Then Mr. Pearson decided to bring Chante back to live with him and his new mate, Alex Dixon. Alex started out being nice, considerate and understanding. They had moved into a new apartment and Alex had fixed up a bedroom for her.

He got her registered into a new school and if you can, believe it or not, he was the one that got her into church and baptized. But slowly, things began to change. Alex began to drink more and his demeanor began to change also. Chante even noticed that her grand-

5

father had started to change and shortly after an incident, Chante began to be withdrawn.

Alex was a man who played the woman of the house. *I give it to him—he was good at cooking, cleaning and all the basic domestic roles.* He was even good at doing hair, but deep down inside of him there was a whole different person. Alex was a tall, light-skinned man with receding hair. *I'm not going to say that he was a private person because when he started drinking, privacy went out the window. You see back in the early sixties, gayness was kept in the closet, not like how it is today. No one has the right to judge you except God. Alex could drink all week long and then go to church on Sunday, sing and shout, then by Monday, he would be back to being deceitful and hateful.*

I remember hanging out with Chante, and Alex would come outside on one of his drinking binges with a wig and earrings. Chante would look so embarrassed. If Mr. Pearson were out there, he would just get up and go into his apartment.

I really think that it was very selfish of him to get up and leave his granddaughter out there to face all the ridicules and laughter from some of the other tenants, kids and neighbors on the block.

When Alex was having a good day, he would take Chante to the zoo, shopping, and occasionally out to eat. *I know for a fact that Chante enjoyed going to church because it was one of the few places that she could forget about her dysfunctional home life.* After a while, Mr. Pearson and Alex stopped going to church as often, which was better for Chante because they had taught her to go by herself. Now, don't think for one minute that church people don't gossip, too. It was easier when they stopped going because then Chante didn't have to hear some of the little comments that people made.

I do believe that everyone gets a chance to redeem themselves. We all have sins and we have to repent for them, but some people refuse to change the bad things about themselves and continue to put the blame on others. We are accountable for our own actions.

For a while, things seem to be going pretty good in the Pearson household until an incident when child protection was called because of a gash going down the front of Chante's head. *I guess now you want me to tell you what happened?*

Chante had come home from school and no one was home. Chante was not allowed to have a key to the apartment. So one day after school, her grandfather was at work and Alex was nowhere to be found. So like any other day, Mr. Pearson had called home as he usually did every day to check and make sure Chante was in the house. So when he called and got no answer, he called an upstairs neighbor—Mrs. Finley—and asked if she would go down and check to see if Chante was in the hallway. She was, and Mrs. Finley informed her that her grandfather wanted to speak to her on the phone. Mrs. Finley had watched after her a few times when her grandfather and Alex had to go out, so she knew it was okay. Mr. Pearson told Chante to stay with Mrs. Finley until one of them got home.

Well, Alex came home very intoxicated that day and was outraged that Chante was not in the hallway. So when Mrs. Finley heard him in the hallway, she tried to explain the conversation that transpired with Mr. Pearson, but Alex wasn't listening. He charged into Mrs. Finley's apartment and snatched the bat and ball paddle that Chante was playing with and hit her in the head.

Now you would think that something was done about that; well think again—the very next day, Alex's clothes and personal belongings were hidden so that when child protection came they would see that no one lived there but Chante and her grandfather.

Chante was shipped off again and this time, it was for a long time and she was only allowed to come home when William came to visit.

Sometimes you have to sit back and wonder what could go so wrong in a person's life to make them act and do certain things. Chante would return home about a year and a half later, and as she started to get much older, she was embarrassed about people knowing that she lived with two men; but she could not express her concerns because who would listen to a child?

Chapter 4

DADDY

Exodus 13:12, "Honour thy father and thy mother that thy days may be long upon the land which the Lord thy God giveth thee."

I know by now you are wondering: who is William? Why did Chante always have to come home when he came to visit? Well, let me see if I can explain.

William Harris was only known as Chante's biological father. Okay. Okay! I know you are thinking that Charles Lewis was her father.

Nobody knows exactly when Deidre started seeing William, but when she found out she was pregnant, she thought that it was a strong possibility that Chante was his but the child was given Charles's last name. No father was ever named on the birth certificate. *I heard that the reason was because William had been married at the time. Now this was happening back in the sixties.*

So while Chante was growing up, she only knew about William—not knowing there was even another man involved until her mother's death. Meanwhile, William was a good dad. He tried to make sure that she had everything that she needed. Until he found out that the money that he was providing was not going toward Chante but to Alex instead. William stopped sending money for clothes—instead, he would go get her and take her himself. He did everything in his power to make sure that she knew that he loved her and he was sorry that he could not raise her himself, so he tried to make it up in different ways.

Chante would shine whenever she talked about her dad. He was a very responsible and hardworking family man. He never hid the fact that he had a daughter out of the marriage. Chante was brought around them from time to time, starting from an infant whenever it was possible for William to get her.

William's family never made her feel like an outsider even if they were thinking it. She was brought up knowing his biological kids with his wife as her sisters and brothers. Chante used to say her father loved working on cars, houses, or just sitting on his porch shooting the breeze with family and friends.

I know for a fact that Chante really enjoyed the time that she did get to spend with her father. She clung to that genuine love that William gave her. But soon, she would cling on to that love more tightly because she was about to become a motherless child.

Chapter 5

TRAGEDY HITS HOME

John 11:25–26, "I am the resurrection, and the light: he that believeth in me, though he were dead, yet shall he live. And whosoever liveth and believeth in me shall never die."

In this cynical world today, a lot of children and adults do not realize how precious it is to have a mother. You should always be able to think of your mom with warm and cherished feelings. Part of Chante's mom problems was that she wanted acceptance from her father, and ever since she had become pregnant with her first child, their relationship had went downhill. Mr. Pearson seems to be filled with hatred for his daughter.

During the years, Deidre seem to sink deeper into drinking. She would seem to get into relationships with men that didn't want to love her, but only to blacken her eyes and bust her lips. Meanwhile, her very own father thought that it was what she deserved.

On the day of Deidre's death, that morning in November, was a stormy overcast. The sky had an extremely dark and cloudy appearance and though it had not started raining, it was such an eerie looking day.

When Chante got home from school that evening, Mr. Pearson was already standing at the apartment door waiting for her with a solemn look on his face. He told Chante to put away her schoolbooks and come into the dining room. When she got into the dining room, she noticed her grandfather had tears in his eyes and she had never seen him shed a tear before. Mr. Pearson started talking about how things were rough and unstable for her older sister Saprina who had somehow gotten back with Deidre. He continued in saying that he had tried to do the best he could in trying to raise her, and after five minutes of patting himself on the back, he finally told her that her mother had died and that she had been killed by her live-in partner. At that moment, Chante really didn't know how to react. She really didn't know how she was supposing to feel, but soon her emotions naturally took over and she cried. She cried because she was never allowed to talk to or visit her mother.

She cried for the mother that she would never get to know. She cried for feeling like the only child in the world without a mother. She cried harder at the fact that while she sat watching her grandfather crying, she felt he had no right to cry. How could he sit there and dare cry when he would barely acknowledge her? How could he cry when he was the one that abandoned his wife and kids?

Chapter 6

THE FIASCO

Isaiah 41:10, "Fear thou not: for I am with thee: be not dismayed; for I am thy God: I will strengthen thee; yea, I will help thee; yea, I will uphold thee with the right hand of my righteousness."

When Deidre passed away, Mr. Pearson had her body sent down the country for this is where she would be buried. So he had the morticians bring the hearse with the body in it, to pick up Alex and Chante. Mr. Pearson would drive down later.

I never understood the philosophy behind wanting your grandchild to ride in a hearse, but that's what he did.

As the morticians got out of the hearse in front of Mr. Pearson's apartment building, they were informed that they would be taking Alex and Chante with them. The gentlemen were quite baffled by this, but they agreed. They suggested that Chante sit up front so that she would not be afraid. But, oh no! Mr. Pearson saw it differently. Chante was to sit in the back with Alex and her mother's remains. Now this really petrified Chante, and she started to cry because even though the deceased was her mother, the child was only ten and she was terrified and should not have been riding in a hearse at all.

On this day, most of the tenants had come outside to give their support and they could not believe what Mr. Pearson was doing. But then again, they could not believe that two men got away with raising a little girl. So as Mr. Pearson was trying to convince Chante

12

to get in, he was threatening that if she didn't stop embarrassing him and didn't get in the hearse, he was going to beat her behind and make her stay home while everyone went to the funeral. Everyone around seemed shocked at this—even the morticians—so they tried to defuse the situation by suggesting that Mr. Pearson allow Chante to sit up front. Mr. Pearson did not like that solution too much, but he finally agreed. So finally, they got on the road and the trip took about four hours. Chante felt a little better about riding up front instead in the back. When they reached the funeral home in Chapel Hill, another mortician came out and removed the body, and some of Mr. Pearson's family members were there to pick up Alex and Chante. Now most of the members in this family could not stand Alex, but they just tolerated him because of Mr. Pearson and Chante.

Deidre's casket was sky blue and she was laid to rest in a pink negligee. *I never did understand that either, and neither had I ever seen it before. Alex did her hair and he also prepared the program and the family paper. The family thought this whole situation was some kind of sick joke. How could this man that seemed to despise his own daughter let his lover run the show? What a show!*

During the funeral, Mr. Pearson sobbed like no tomorrow. Chante found out that she had two more sisters and another father. If you think that's bad enough, Alex went into a seizure while reading the obituary and he passed out knocking over the flowers and almost tipping over the casket.

I always say you can't be in God's house being ugly. After getting to the cemetery, Mr. Pearson was so shaken up with grief or guilt, whichever the case maybe, that he almost collapsed into the grave along with his daughter. He might have wished it was that easy, but unfortunately, he would have to do a little more suffering before he went to his grave.

Now before everyone departed to go back to their normal lives, Chante did get to meet her older sister Alexis. She didn't get to see Amanda because she had pneumonia and could not make it. Finally, after all these years, Charles had resurfaced as he was there, too. When it came to Charles, Chante had never seen or heard of him and she could not comprehend why was her grandfather telling her not to call William daddy while she was here. So when Charles came over to say hello and introduce himself to Chante, she was really confused. You see, Charles had not seen any of his children since they were taken away from him and Deidre ten years ago.

After Deidre was laid to rest, the trial for her murder got underway and the person responsible only got five years.

Sometimes I think after Chante lost her mother—although she didn't live with her—she felt as if a part of her was gone, too. I really think after that she got more into church.

Chapter 7

A Place Where There Is Joy

Psalms 150:16, "Let everything that hath breath praise the Lord."

One good thing that Alex did for Chante was placing her name on the church role. During her young life, she would find out that the joy of going to the Lord's house would have a great impact on her life. Believe it or not when Alex enrolled her in the church, he was still very active. He sang on two choirs and helped in the church kitchen.

Chante's favorite part about church was the convocation. There were lots of singing and preaching. Buses would come from cities far and near for the annual baptism. It was a week of praising the Lord. As Chante got older, people would always make fun of her about going to church, but she didn't let that deter her. She felt if people could go to the nightclubs and party for the devil, why was it so strange to go to church and dance for the Lord? Sometimes, things are a bit strange and unusual when we don't understand them.

Chante really enjoyed going to church and she began to sing on the choir. She tried to participate in all the services and at the age of fifteen, during one of the revival services, she became saved. This would become her strength to try and endure everything that came her way.

Sometimes, going to church with Alex got to be more embarrassing than joy. Sometimes, he would decide to go when he had been drinking and some of the members noticed. Mr. Pearson seldom went to church. He would drop them off and come back and pick them up.

When Chante turned around sixteen, neither Alex nor her grandfather went to church anymore. Alex had started drinking more and Mr. Pearson just sat at home; in fact, she preferred them not to go. She had found a Godmother within the church that had took her under her wing.

I, for one, am really happy that she found peace with being baptized, saved, and really finding a personal connection with God. I am also glad that the church was there for her because it would help teach, mold and save Chante's life and sanity. I know a lot of times she truly didn't understand a lot of things in the Bible, but as she grew into adult years, things would later come to pass; and because of the time that she spent inside the church with the preaching and teachings, that would stay with her as she matured.

As these next few years go by, you will see that the church was truly her strength. Things are not about to get easier, oh no. Now this may be a good time to get something to drink, or maybe a snack, because things are about to get real crazy.

Chapter 8

No One to Tell

Romans 5:19, "For as by one man's disobedience many were made sinners, so by the obedience of one shall many be made righteous."

Sometimes during the summer months, Chante was allowed to spend a couple of weeks with her grandmother. One summer in particular, Chante was out playing with her cousins and she had gotten thirsty, so she went into the house to get something to drink. One of her cousins asked if he could go with her because he wanted to stop by and see Gerard, who was Mr. Pearson's youngest son, who had muscular dystrophy and was confined to the bed. So Chante didn't think anything about it because she had often stayed down Bruce's house with her other cousins.

After going in the house, Chante proceeded to go downstairs to the kitchen to get something to drink, leaving Bruce upstairs with Gerard. After putting her glass in the sink, as she turned around, she was startled because Bruce was directly behind her. Chante had not heard him come downstairs. She had never felt a reason to be afraid of him because of all the times they had been around each other. But what he did next would change her world forever.

He grabbed her and threw her down on the dining room floor and started snatching off her underwear. When she tried to scream, he put his hand over her mouth and proceeded to take her virginity.

As Chante cried and tried to plead for him to stop, Bruce seem to be in another world—the only thing that stopped him was when the front door opened and he heard someone come in. He then looked at Chante and told her that she had better not tell anyone, and then he went out the back door.

Chante was so frightened and scared that she didn't know what to do, so she fixed her clothes and went upstairs as if nothing had happened. She really wanted to tell someone, but she felt afraid because she knew that her grandfather would have to be told and he would beat her and blame everything on her. She also knew if her grandfather found out that she would never get to come to her grandmother's house again. Chante felt that there was no one to tell about this because they would definitely go tell her grandfather.

I think, deep down Chante was afraid that Bruce would get into trouble and the whole family would blame her because he was one of the family's favorite.

If only someone had took the time and taught her that no one has the right to violate your body; that it is wrong no matter who it was and it should have been reported. Chante felt she had no one to tell or to talk to. Because of this horrible incident in her life, it would be a long time before she ever learned to trust and when she did, it would be for the wrong reasons.

To this day, I don't think no one in the family ever knew about that day and Chante lived with that horrible nightmare. When she finally did break down and told someone, it would be the wrong kind of person and they would throw that up at her every chance they got.

Proverbs 22:6, "Train a child in the way he should go."

The Bible says, "When I was a child, I spoke as a child, I understand as a child, I thought as a child, but when I became a woman, I put away childish things." Chante never got the chance to really enjoy her childhood. So when Sister Brown came into her life, it helped by having a mother figure.

Sister Brown was also a member of the same church that Chante attended. She was a stern person but not as strict as Alex and Mr. Pearson. Sister Brown didn't live too far away so she would ask if

Chante could spend the weekend with her sometimes. Mr. Pearson really liked Sister Brown and he knew she would keep her eyes on Chante, and if she got out of line he knew that she would tell him, at least that's what he thought.

After a while, people at church sort of forgot about Mr. Pearson and they sort of took it as if Sister Brown was Chante's mother. Sister Brown would take her just about everywhere she went to get her out of the house. So during her teenage years, when you saw Sister Brown, you saw Chante. There was also something else going on that was not supposed to be happening: Chante had a boyfriend. Sister Brown knew about Chante and Brandon but she did not tell Mr. Pearson about them. The good thing was that Chante was starting to mingle with people her age, but she was also beginning to be interested in other things that Brandon had to offer.

Sister Brown liked Brandon, but she was very leery about his intentions with Chante. She would always tell Chante to be careful with him and not to do anything to get herself into trouble.

I wish for once that she had heeded to those words because that's where she was headed and it would take church and God to really bring her through.

Chapter 9

SWEET SIXTEEN

Proverbs 8:17, "I love them that love me; and those that seek me early shall find me."

I remember a very embarrassing episode that happened on Chante's sixteenth birthday that really stood out. Every year, Alex and Mr. Pearson gave Chante a birthday party. This was one of those rare times that she was allowed to have friends over. So this particular year it should have been a special time because she was turning sweet sixteen. They had let her invite a few of her school and neighborhood friends over.

Recently, they had just found out that she had a boyfriend, and believe it or not they let him come, too. Now it really was a long time before Alex and Mr. Pearson found out about Chante and Brandon. The reason that they found out was because Chante had asked her father William to but a gift for a boy at church because they had a secret Santa at choir rehearsal and she had gotten Brandon's name; but when William came to visit, he had asked her about Brandon. Mr. Pearson was astonished about Chante wanting to get a gift for a boy. Believe it or not, because he knew that Brandon was from the church and he also knew Brandon's grandmother who sung on the same choir with Alex, he agreed with William that it was okay.

Now it would have been a different matter if William was not involved. There would have not been a gift for no boy.

Crystal and Brandon's friendship blossomed into a real relationship or something. We'll get into that later. So to celebrate Chante's sixteenth birthday, Alex brought out the good china that they only used on special occasions. He cooked as usual, and made the birthday cake. It was three layers, and mind you, Alex had been drunk when he made this cake. It was pretty on the outside with the icing and the candles and tore up on the inside.

While everyone was standing singing happy birthday, Alex handed Chante a knife to cut the cake. Well, when that child sliced down the center of that cake the inside started oozing out. It started coming out from the middle and then the whole cake started collapsing and sinking.

Chante's face turned from happiness to embarrassment. She actually wanted to crawl underneath the table and die. Alex had cooked the cake with pudding mixed in the batter and it was not fully done. Mr. Pearson pretended as if he was mad but sometimes when it came to Alex, it was hard to tell what he was feeling. Chante's grandfather let everyone finish eating their ice cream, and then the party was over and they had to go home.

After everyone left, Chante just sit in her room crying and listening to Mr. Pearson and Alex arguing over the cake. Soon afterward, Chante started really growing strong animosity toward Alex. Unfortunately, things were about to get worse because she was about to take a giant leap right out of the flying pan into the fire, and she definitely was going to get burnt.

Chapter 10

CAUGHT UP

Leviticus 10:10, "And that ye may put difference between holy and unholy, and between clean and unclean."

After Chante's sixteenth birthday, her and Brandon's relationship began to get stronger. I'm not too sure that was a good thing because things were changing. Chante had started skipping school to hang out with Brandon and her grades were starting to slip.

During the last few months of the summer, Chante had noticed that she hadn't seen her period and she had been throwing up a lot. She tried to keep this from being noticed at home, but Alex had also noticed that when Chante came home from school, she also slept a lot and this was something she never did. So he thought it was time to bring this to the attention of Mr. Pearson. Now upon hearing this new information, he was not happy at all so immediately he called the family doctor and set up an appointment for the next morning. When Chante heard her grandfather on the phone, she knew there was no way that she was about to get out of this one. You see, Brandon and Chante already had an idea that she was pregnant and they both knew that when her grandfather found out, the gates of hell were going to open and swallow them whole. Brandon tried to assure Chante that everything would be all right, but Chante knew that nothing would ever be the same again. Frankly, she was quite scared.

So the next morning, Alex and Chante went to the doctors and yes, the results were that she was three months along. On the way home, Chante tried of thinking of ways to get away from Alex and run away, but where would she go? When Alex and Chante got off the bus, there was Mr. Pearson standing on the front porch of the building waiting. He had already gotten the report from the doctor and was very angry. As soon as Chante got close to him, he just hauled off and slapped the taste out of her. He told her to get in the house because he was going to beat that bastard child right out of her, and then she was going to be sent away to a place that no one would ever see her again. *Believe me when I tell you that exactly what he tried to do and after that beating, he let her know that she would have no more contact with Brandon. He also informed her that the next morning she would be going to have an abortion and there was nothing that no one could do about it.*

After Mr. Pearson and Alex left the apartment, Chante snuck a call to Brandon to let him know what her grandfather had said. Brandon could not believe what her grandfather was going through with making her have an abortion; and he wanted his child, so he tried to convince Chante not to worry—that everything would be all right—but that fell on deaf ears because she knew that things would never be the same again.

Later that night, Brandon's grandmother called Mr. Pearson and tried to convince him that her grandson wanted his baby and he would marry her even though they both were too young, and Mr. Pearson would have to sign the papers to allow the marriage because Chante was only sixteen. He didn't hesitate—it was either that or an abortion.

Chapter 11

A STRANGE PLACE

Deuteronomy 5:17, "Thou shalt not kill."

On that following morning, Alex took Chante to the abortion clinic. They went into a strange-looking building that had no name on the front. The building had an eerie feeling to it. After Alex gave the nurse Chante's name and finished filling out the forms, she was quickly taken into a room in the back. She was asked to put on a hospital gown and to wait for the doctor's arrival. While waiting for the doctor, Chante noticed a partition on the other side of the room and she remember seeing a doctor with some kind of strange device doing something to another patient. She remembers hearing the lady crying and hollering out in pain and this frightened her.

When the doctor finally came into the room where she was, he gave her another pelvic examination and questioned her about her pregnancy. He asked her if she was definitely sure that she wanted to get rid of her baby because by his examination, she was further along than she had previously been told. Now Chante was kind of glad that she was too far along and she informed the doctor that she had not wanted the abortion, but it was her grandfather that was making her have it. The doctor informed her that no one could make her have an abortion and because of his examination, he was by law, not able to perform the procedure. He then told her to get dressed and he would inform her guardian that was with her.

Well, you know that when Chante got home, Mr. Pearson was not happy at all about the news that she did not get the abortion. It was that night that the biggest and hardest decision of Chante's life would take place. You see, Mr. Pearson also collected every month on money for Chante from William, and he was getting a SSI check for her too. So he really didn't want to see that extra money get cut off because she decided to get knocked up fast. He really was thinking hard about not letting her make the decision of marriage or abortion. He could just send her right up to New York for a day with Alex and it would be over with . . .

Chapter 12

Decisions

Psalm 37:37, "Mark the perfect man, and behold the upright: for the end of that man is peace."

Everyone makes decisions in some point of their lives. Sometimes, you make good ones and sometimes you make bad ones. Chante was put in the kind of predicament where a sixteen year-old should have never been made to make. It was a decision that her grandfather gave her to make that would affect the rest of her life.

First of all, she was naive to the outside world. It was a lot of things that she had no idea about or understood. She barely could understand what was going on in her own home. Mr. Pearson gave Chante the ultimate decision that either she get married to Brandon, or be sent to a home for unwed mothers. Now, if she chose not to get married and went to the home for unwed mothers, after the baby was born, she would be sent away and no one would see her again until she turned eighteen. Mr. Pearson was determined that he was not having any embarrassment brought to his home. He had the nerve to say that he didn't want the neighbors and his family to see him as a failure. *Well, I think the neighbors and his family already had their opinion of him. Then again, I think it was a little too late to be worrying what anybody thought. Don't you?*

So in 1976, Chante and Brandon was married at the church that they both attended. Chante was by now almost six months pregnant and lucky for her, she carried her pregnancy well and was not show-ing much. But it almost came close not being a wedding because of the incident the night before the wedding. Here's what happened: Alex was pressing Chante's hair and he had been drinking all day. He started burning Chante badly with the straightening comb and when she started to complain, he slapped her across the face and when he did that, Chante took her foot and kicked him so hard that if it had not been for Mr. Pearson catching him in time, he would have hit the window. Mr. Pearson was very upset behind that episode and he made Chante go to bed. He said that he was going to cancel the wed-ding but he didn't; instead, he and Alex got into a heated argument over the fact that Chante was pregnant and how she was a disgrace just like her mother.

Chapter 13

Out of the Frying Pan and into the Fire

Hebrews 13:4, "Marriage is honorable in all, and the bed defiled; but whoremongers and adulterers God will judge."

Most of Chante's and Brandon's friends, family and congregation were in attendance for their wedding. There were people there that were just being plain nosy. There were a lot of spectators there that really thought that the young couple should not be getting married. Some people were even heard saying, "this marriage was doomed for failure before it even got started." Even though they were probably right, they should have kept their opinions to themselves.

Mr. Pearson got them a small room around the corner from him. They stayed with an elderly couple that had another family member staying there that was mentally challenged he had a habit of peeking through their keyhole to their room. So after a couple of months, they were able to move into another apartment across the street. Mr. Pearson also knew the elderly lady that owned the house. The landlady was a strange woman. She always kept her shades drawn and she always wore black. To make sure no one stole her money, she kept it pinned and rolled up in her stockings.

Things were changing quickly and the couple were not adapting to the changes of marriage too well. You see, Chante was not use to having to cook, to clean and have sexual relations on a daily basis. Brandon was not really prepared to take care of a wife and provide for a household. Since Chante was only sixteen and pregnant, she could not get a job; so Brandon was responsible to take care of both of them.

Most of the time, they ate at church because Brandon's grandmother worked in the church kitchen. And other than that, they both slept during the day because at that time Brandon did not have a job and Chante had dropped out of school.

Months into Chante's pregnancy, things got very chaotic. Mr. Pearson and Alex were constantly in their business and trying to bad-mouth them to anyone that would listen to them. Then there was Brandon's side of the family trying to give them their opinion. Soon it just seemed like everyone was trying to tell them what to do at one time, but the two sides were clashing.

On the day that Chante went into labor, Brandon's family had given her a baby shower but what they didn't know was that the day before, Chante had woke up with urges to go to the bathroom and since she felt no pain, she thought nothing of it; so like everything else that happened in her life, she kept it to herself. So the next day during the baby shower she finally confided in someone that she could not stop going to the bathroom. Well, guess what? Chante was indeed in labor minus the pain, which was a good thing. Come to find out she had been in active labor and her water had been broke for twenty-four hours. She was then rushed to Washington Hospital Center and admitted immediately.

During the next several hours, Chante was monitored closely but it seemed like she just would not dilate. So at about ten o'clock, the doctors decided that she would have a C-section, and at ten fifty-six a.m., Darvrin Winters was born beautiful and healthy.

Chapter 14

PROBLEMS, PROBLEMS, AND MORE PROBLEMS

Matthew 19:14, "But Jesus said, suffer little children and forbid them not to come unto me for of such is the kingdom of heaven."

In 1977, the couple was blessed with their daughter. There were plenty of family and friends around to meet the addition with the exception of two people who were extremely upset and those were Mr. Pearson and Alex.

Chante's grandfather was highly upset because he felt that he should have been the first one called when it was time for her to go to the hospital instead of her father William. Now Alex was upset because the nurses would not let him hold the baby in the nursery. So by the time they got into Chante's room, they were heated and they wanted to start a big commotion, but the nurses intervened and told them they had to leave.

Four months later after Chante and Brandon were trying to adapt to having a new baby, plus Brandon had not found work yet, things went terribly wrong. Chante really still had no idea how to care for a home—let alone an infant child—and mind you, she was pretty much still a child herself. Both sides of the family were trying to help and give their advice, but neither side had the same advice.

Mainly, Mr. Pearson, who was still very angry over the hospital sit-uation, he was determined that Chante had to do things his way or no way at all. He had sent word that he wanted Chante to come see him by herself so that he could talk to her about something very important. So she decided to take her daughter with her because maybe it was good time for her grandfather to spend some time with his great-grandchild.

When Chante got to her grandfather's house, he immediately jumped on her over the fact that William was called to the hospital before he was. Chante tried to explain to him that she was not the one that called her father and that she really did not understand why it was so much of a big issue. Well, that was not a good enough answer; Mr. Pearson felt she should have made sure that she called him before she even went to the hospital. If that was not bad enough, he made it worse by bringing up the fact that Alex had not been allowed into the nursery to hold the baby and this was also Chante's fault. Chante again tried to explain that she had no control over hospital policy.

Mr. Pearson didn't except that answer either. He then turned to Chante and said, "You need to give me that baby because you and Brandon don't need any kids." Chante was shocked. You see, she had always seen how heartless he was, but she never thought that some-thing like that would come out of his mouth. Then he had the nerve to say, "I tried to get your mother to listen and you are acting just like her, and you will end up like her, too."

Chante, with tears streaming down her face, picked up her daughter and held her tightly, but her grandfather had one more threat. He said, "Either you give that baby to me, or I will see that she is taken away for good."

As Chante was on her way home from the hospital, she really feared that her grandfather would carry out his threat. So she had waited until she got home to tell Brandon all that had taken place. He was very upset. He stormed out of the house to the nearest tele-phone to give Mr. Pearson a call. Mr. Pearson told him the same exact thing that he had told Chante and that infuriated Brandon more. He then went back into the house and wrote Mr. Pearson a very angry letter that expressed how he felt about Mr. Pearson and Alex trying to take his child away.

The very next week, all hell broke loose when the child protection agency showed up. It really turned out not to be a pleasant visit at all.

I really think this was truly the downfall in a marriage that was truly doomed from the start.

I also think that all the anger of getting married too young and having a child was too much for the young couple. They were really not prepared for all the trials and tribulations and most of all, the responsibilities. Believe me when I tell you that things were about to become a nightmare.

Chapter 15

Please Wake Me from This Nightmare

Hebrews 11:6, "For he that cometh to God must believe that he is, and that he is a rewarder of them that diligently seek him."

1977 seemed like a torturous year for Chante and Brandon. After the not-so-pleasant visit from the children protection agency, things seem to spiral out of control quickly. Now don't forget that Chante is sixteen about to turn seventeen at this time, and Brandon is around twenty-one.

Like I said before, they were not ready for marriage or a child. There were a lot of changes happening quickly and also a lot of people had a lot to say about the whole situation. Sometimes, I wonder if some of those people had spoken up when she was being raised by two men who was mentally and physically abusing her, maybe things would have turned out differently. So where were those people that had so much to say then?

Brandon had started to get a little controlling and his rule was, "you do as I say because I'm the man of the house." It seemed as if Brandon wanted to pick out the clothes that Chante wore, her friends that she was allowed to be around, and where she could and could not go. Chante was not at all happy with the sudden change in Brandon's demeanor. She thought that she had escaped all of that when she left her grandfather's house.

Chante seemed also to not be adapting too well to any of these new changes. First of all, she was still a child herself. She never was allowed to go out with people her own age without her grandfather's permission, so most of the people she did know was people in school who teased her, people at church who sometimes seemed to pity her, and occasional visits with her father and grandmother whom her grandfather monitored. She didn't have to cook because Alex took care of that and didn't want anyone in his kitchen. She only had to clean her bedroom because Alex did the rest.

I know someone out there is thinking, "well, she knew how to get a baby." Well that's your opinion so did you? Chante was sheltered, naive and oblivious to the real outside world.

In this life when you sometimes think that every time someone gives you a smile that they are a good person, that is not always true.

Chapter 16

ONCE WAS NOT ENOUGH

Now there was one thing that Chante missed other than her daughter, and that was her family. She did get the pleasure of her father stopping by occasionally, but she felt she was drifting away from the rest. Even though Chante was trying to focus on the new baby, she just felt so angry all the time. Sometimes she felt angry because she was not the one to see her daughter take her very first steps. She was not there to hear her say mommy for the first time. She felt that all those special moments in a mother's life went to someone else and it hurt. Chante felt that she was still in no position to do anything about it and the guilt was eating her up on the inside. Here, they were again about to have a second child who was a blessing, but they could still barely take care of themselves.

The good thing about this time was that Brandon did have a job in security and he seemed to be happy with the job. So Chante hoped that it would ease some of the tension and stress that was eating away at their marriage. This time around, Chante was determined to be a better mother and do better with her wifely duties that she had done the first time around.

Chante also wanted to go back to school, get a job and some integrity about herself. She knew it was not going to be easy but if God kept his loving arms wrapped around her, she would make it.

Not only was she willing to come out of her shell of uncertainty, but she really wanted to work on that rage that seem to keep boiling deep down inside.

Chapter 17

TRYING

Romans 9:25, "But if we hope for that we see not, then do we with patience wait for it."

In March 1978, Chantelle Winters made her debut into the world by way of C- section. She was beautiful and healthy just like her older sisters.

Chante had a lot of visitors with the exception of her grandfather and Alex who was still mad at her. Deep down inside she wished her grandfather could show her some love instead of so much animosity. As usual her father William was there which always made her smile. Even though he was still not pleased about the situation, he showed her support and love through every birth.

After Chante brought Chantelle home, she began to put more effort on her domestic and motherly skills. She even tried her hand at preparing a meal for Brandon's family that really turned out well. But there were some things new starting to tear at her. Chante started to feel like Brandon's family showed favoritism toward Darvrin and left Chantelle out. She did not want to think that way, but it seemed like she could not control that feeling and with this brought on more resentment toward the family.

I think that if she could truly have found someone that she could trust to listen to her, it would have helped. Sometimes, God brings people into your life for a reason because soon after Chantelle was born, Chante met Jocelyn McCormick. *Jocelyn lived down the street with her boyfriend and five kids. Chante and Jocelyn were almost in the same predicament. They both felt that they had men that just wanted to keep them barefoot and pregnant, like the old saying goes.*

Chante and Jocelyn became real good friends. They were able to confide in each other over their feelings and situations. *I think this friendship was really good for Chante because she got to see how loving and attentive Jocelyn was with all five of her kids, despite of her situation with her man. Chante wanted to be that way with her own children.*

So Chante did more cleaning and cooking. She did much better at tending to Chantelle but something was still missing.

She felt like her grandfather hated her. She felt like a stranger in her oldest daughter's life even though she wasn't. She also realized that she held so much anger and she really needed to get rid of it because this, too, was not healthy. Chante wanted so much to make peace with her grandfather and try and build a more loving relationship with her two year-old.

No matter how much she tried not to show it around Brandon's family, she was just angry.

I really think it was because she felt that her own family no longer loved her. She felt overwhelmed and mostly like a disgrace to them. I think she would have seen that most of them really didn't feel like that. If she had not been ashamed to go around them, I also feel that she would not have had these insecurities. If her grandfather had not put those thoughts in her head, she wouldn't have so low self-esteem. Maybe it was time for her to pay her grandfather a visit.

Chapter 18

THE VISIT

Luke 6:37, "Judge not and ye shall not be judged; condemn not and ye shall not be condemned; forgive and ye shall be forgiven."

On a nice but cloudy day, Chante decided that she wanted bygones be bygones and let her grandfather see his newest great-grandchild for whom he had not had the pleasure of seeing because of the big fallout over Darvrin. Chante had not spoken or visited his apartment since. She felt that it was time to try and make peace, but Brandon was not so happy to oblige. Really, you could not blame him.

Somehow, Chante convinced Brandon to let her go and take Chantelle. *I also think that his grandmother may have had a hand in helping with persuading him to let them go. His grandmother knew all about the confrontation with Brandon and Mr. Pearson, but she figured that it was time to try and make amends. So Chante wrapped up her daughter and took the thirty-minute ride to see her grandfather.*

Chante was a little leery about going to see her grandfather. She remembered very well what transpired on that last visit and the events that took place afterward but she was determined to conquer her fears and to try anyway.

When Chante got to the apartment building, many of the tenants were sitting outside on the stoop. One person was Mrs. Jamison.

Mrs. Jamison was a loving elderly lady that lived down the hall from Mr. Pearson with her cousin and her pet dog Blackie. Mrs. Jamison was really glad to see Chante and she was very anxious to see the new addition, but because she had the dog with her and she didn't want him to jump on Chante with the baby in her arms, she told her that she would meet her at her grandfather's. Chante felt a bit relief knowing that someone would be in the apartment with her.

Once Chante got into her grandfather's apartment, she felt very uncomfortable especially when he asked to hold Chantelle; but she gave in and let him. Alex was still lingering around but no matter how hard Chante tried to shake the feeling, she just did not feel comfortable and neither did she feel safe.

Chante was thinking that maybe she should just leave because her grandfather got right back on the subject of wanting to take her baby again, but before he could really get going, Mrs. Jamison knocked on the door.

It felt as if God sent an angel to intervene. Mr. Pearson was not pleased about Mrs. Jamison coming to visit Chante. He also let her know that he did not appreciate her coming around. Mrs. Jamison was shocked at what had come out of his mouth. She told him that she did not know that he had a problem with her coming to see Chante and the baby.

As Mrs. Jamison prepared to leave after holding Chantelle, she let Chante know that it had started to rain and asked if she had cab fare to get home instead of being in the rain with the baby waiting on the bus. When Chante told her that she didn't, Mr. Pearson told Mrs. Jamison that she needed to mind her own business and there was nothing wrong with Chante catching the bus. He then told her that if Chante had done what he told her to do and given the baby to him, she wouldn't have to stand in the rain; but since she wanted to be stubborn, then he didn't care what happened to her or the child.

Mrs. Jamison could not believe this man and she feared for Chante and the baby if she left them, so she told Chante to wrap up her baby and she was going to send her home in a cab. After that day, Chante never went back to visit again; and shortly after, Mr. Pearson became gravely ill and passed away months later.

Chapter 19

SISTERS FINALLY MEET

Matthew 15:11, "Not that which goeth into the mouth defileth a man; but that which cometh out of the mouth, this defileth a man."

During the death of Chante's grandfather, Chante was going through hard times. Again, Chante was put into a predicament of making the decision about the welfare of her second daughter Chantelle, but this time it had nothing to do with children services.

Chante had finally gotten herself a job and was very happy about working; but Brandon wanted all the money to go to him and Chante was having a serious problem with that. So again she made the decision because of all the issues going on in the home to get Chantelle out of harm's way until she could figure out what to do. So it was during this time that Mr. Pearson passed away. When Chante got the news, she really didn't know how react. She knew she felt sad but she also felt some relief, and she didn't quite understand why she felt that way.

The funeral was held in a small country town known as Clarksville, Virginia. Chante and Brandon had ridden down with her aunt and grandmother. Upon arriving at the family house where everyone was meeting, Chante was greeted by her Aunt Agnes and she had two young ladies with her. Chante had no idea who they were, but she knew that they were part of the family. Never would she have expected to hear her aunt say that these were her sisters, Amanda and Alexis.

Chante was overjoyed at meeting her sisters even though she wished it had been a different occasion, but it was a pleasure just the same. Before going to the funeral, the three sisters got to spend some quality time together; they went away from the family and got to know each other, but there was still one sister missing, Saprina. Alexis had told Chante that they had seen each other before at their mother's funeral, and Amanda had been sick at the time so she had not been able to go. When it was time for the sisters to depart after the funeral, they told Chante that they loved her and they wanted to keep in touch, but that they were also not too keen on her husband. Chante really wanted to break down and tell them all the things that were going on, but she was afraid it would turn into a big confusion and of course, she would get the blame. So she kept up the front and pretended that everything was okay even if it was not.

If you are wondering where was Alex during Mr. Pearson's funeral, he was barred away from the funeral. The family felt they had taken all they could take from him and now that Mr. Pearson was deceased, he was no longer needed to be around.

They had tried to be respectful of all of Mr. Pearson's wishes when he was alive but when he passed away, that's where they drew the line and they firmly stood behind that.

After the funeral, something also changed in Chante. She no longer wanted to feel like a slave in her home or her marriage. She wanted to be able to go around her family and feel that family love that she was missing out on. More importantly she did not want her life to end the way that her mother's did.

Chante had so many things that she wanted to do and she felt that if she stayed in this marriage that she would never accomplish any of them; but just as she was trying to figure things out and get them in order, oops . . .

Chapter 20

NO MORE

Luke 11:19, "And I say unto you, ask and it shall be given; seek and ye shall find; knock and it shall be opened unto you."

Chante felt really good about having a job and only when she went to work and church was she able to feel somewhat normal. She was also still trying to cope with the fact that Brandon's sister was now raising both of her daughters.

I know that Chante was truly grateful for all that they were doing, but it made her feel that because she could not provide and give them a stable home, that she was less than a mother. I really think that seeing her children with someone else and not with their parents was really eating her up inside.

Chante had started feeling extra tired and she did not remember seeing her period. She knew that it was possible to be pregnant because she had not been taking her birth control pills since Brandon had flushed them down the toilet, and when she had gone back to the doctor to get more, he found them and flushed them too.

I always wondered why she was so scared of this man? Why was he allowed to have so much control? What happened to the good times that they had before the marriage?

Anyway, Chante made a doctor's appointment and Brandon decided that this time he would go with her.

When the doctor told them that Chante was indeed pregnant, I really don't think neither was too thrilled but what was done was done. This time they were hoping that they could try a little harder at making this marriage work and eventually have all their children together. I said that's what they thought!

This pregnancy was a little more difficult than the other ones had been. Chante ate all the time. She had picked up a lot of weight and she definitely could not hide it this time. Her blood pressure stayed elevated and this child would also be born by C-section.

During this pregnancy, Chante came to the decisions that she did not want to have any more children. Now Brandon did not like that idea at all. He did not even want to discuss the possibility. Chante's doctor also thought that at the age of twenty-two, she was too young to have her tubes tied, but Chante felt her life could not keep going on in this pattern and something had to change. So she went to her doctor in private and told him some of the things that she was going through and after listening he consented.

So in April 1982, China Winters entered the world. She was a little bit smaller than her other two sisters, but she was healthy and beautiful and that's all that mattered. The important thing is that they had tied her tubes after the delivery of her daughter, and she didn't have to worry about having any more children—which is sort of sad, but it's true.

Chapter 21

ENOUGH

Psalm 25:2, "Oh my God, I trust in thee; let me not be ashamed, let not mine enemies triumph over me."

Things were slowly changing in Chante's marriage. She no longer wanted to live in someone else's house. She knew they were capable of living on their own. She was just tired living in an apartment one minute and getting evicted the next, and it seemed she was the only one to keep a job. Enough was enough and Chante wanted privacy, and she wanted her own place with or without Brandon.

It took a lot of doing, but finally Chante convinced Brandon that they needed to move. So she found a small efficiency apartment that was affordable but big enough for her, Brandon and China. It was a start and because the landlord knew the family, he was willing to work with them. Chante was also happy because her friend Jocelyn lived in the same building. Chante also had started taking classes in the morning to get her GED, and she worked the evening shift at Roy Rogers. She had no problem finding a baby-sitter for China and when she wasn't working and going to school, she took her daughter everywhere with her.

I think Brandon was also noticing the changes in Chante. She seemed to be much happier. She was more protective over China. She had started meeting new friends that Brandon didn't care for and she was starting to be independent. All of a sudden, it looked to Brandon that he

45

was losing control over his wife, but he was determined she would never leave him. Really!

Brandon got so mad about the school situation that he had forbidden her to go. He tore up her books and took away her tokens that the school provided her with. Although she worked, it was just enough to pay the rent and Brandon was no longer working again. At the time, Chante was doing so good in school that she was ready to take the GED test ahead of schedule. She could graduate six months earlier than scheduled. But Brandon was not having any of that. Chante and Brandon had a big argument over the fact that the instructor stopped by to find out why after doing so good, she was not coming to school. Brandon told the instructor that he needed to mind his own business and that his wife did not need a diploma. The instructor was looking at Brandon as if he was crazy so he tried a different approach.

He thought if he could get Brandon to see the advantages of having a GED and that he didn't have to worry about supplying the money for her to get to school because the school provided that for her, maybe he would understand and be proud of his wife for taking this step. Brandon did not want to hear any of that, and he told the instructor that again, Chante was his wife and she was going to do what he said, or else . . .

By that evening, things got really heated and Brandon was determined that Chante was not going to school or nowhere else without his permission. Chante had finally reached her breaking point. She felt she had taken enough physical and mental abuse. She felt she had cried enough tears and she wanted something better for her life, and this marriage was not it. Brandon had gotten so angry with Chante over the school situation that he had taken a swing at her and punched the wall beside her head. Luckily, she moved out of the way just in time. She looked over at her nine-month-old child with tears in her eyes, and knew at that moment she had to make a bold decision. She knew for a fact that Brandon would not let her leave the house with China, so she waited until Brandon seemed to have calmed down a little and ask him if she could go to the store. To keep him from getting suspicious, she asked Jocelyn to go with her.

When Chante and Jocelyn got outside, Chante told her that she had taken enough and she could not go back. She told Jocelyn that she needed her to do her a favor, and to please look after China until the next morning while she found somewhere to stay and then she would come back to get her child. Jocelyn looked at her friend with sadness in her eyes, and told her that she would, but she would not leave her until she knew she was somewhere safe.

Jocelyn knew a friend that lived down the street that would let Chante stay at her house until she could make a decision on what to do next. Chante was more afraid now than ever before but she knew she could not go back and had to move forward. She started so many times that night to change her mind if not so much for her but for her daughter. But deep down, she was afraid that Brandon would beat her to death because she knew by now that he was very angry. All she could do was pray and ask God to protect her daughter, and help her out of this mess that she was in.

Chapter 22

MERCY ME

Matthew 5:7, "Blessed are the merciful for they shall obtain mercy."

The day Chante left Brandon was not easy. Chante had to take off from work to stay hidden from Brandon because she had heard that he had been roaming the neighborhood all night like a mad man. The next morning, Jocelyn had come to tell Chante that Brandon was very angry and he was trying to get information out of her on the whereabouts of Chante, but most of all that China was fine.

Brandy was another friend of Chante's that lived in the building, and she often baby-sat for Chante when she had to work and go to school. Jocelyn told her that Brandon had left China with her that morning, so they went down to get China from Brandy, but when they got there Brandy told Chante that Brandon had come back and picked up China. She said she heard him mention something about taking her to his sister.

By now, Chante was very upset with herself for leaving her daughter in the first place, but she truly felt that was the only way she was going to get away. And she knew in her heart in spite of his feeling about her at the moment that he would never do anything to hurt China. Now he would do everything in his power to keep her away from her daughter and he was going to do everything he could to keep her from getting her.

As the days went on, it was really hard to focus on the GED test that was quickly approaching, but no matter how many streets she had to hide on to keep Brandon away, she was determined to find exactly where her daughter was and take that test.

So one of Chante's co-workers told her that she needed to stop running and go down to the court and get a restraining order, and go to family court and file papers to have Brandon tell her where her child was because he could not keep that information from her. So that's exactly what she did and the courts made a court date immediately for them to come before a judge. While waiting on the courts, Chante had been staying at different place, but in the daytime she hung out with her friend Renee at her house. Renee had a lot of brothers and one of them had taken a liking to Chante, and she had started liking him too. He would come and walk her to work and come back when she got off of work to make sure she made it home safely.

Meanwhile, Chante continued to question family members on the whereabouts of China, but no one wanted to tell her where she was. Finally, a neighbor told her that she had seen Brandon's sister come and get her. Even though Chante had an idea of where China was, she didn't let on to Brandon. She was determined to take him to court and make him give up the information. Two weeks later, a court date was set and they had to meet with the judge. During the questioning, Brandon was very evasive, but the judge was not playing his game. He let him know that if he did not tell where the child was, he would be held for kidnapping. Brandon told the judge that he would tell where China was if Chante told him where she thought the baby was. The judge let Brandon know that this was serious and he could be facing charges, so finally, Brandon decided it was in his best interest to tell where his daughter was. Chante was right all along when she thought that China was with Brandon's sister, which was okay with her—she just wanted her to be safe.

Meanwhile, there was also a restraining order put against Brandon because of many threats.

Chante had found a lawyer that was reasonable so that she could file for a divorce that Brandon said he would never give her. While waiting for her court date, she continued to go to school so that she could take the test to receive her GED.

During the next few weeks, it was very difficult being in the same vicinity that Brandon was in, because he was watching every move that she made. Whenever she came home from work, he was standing out on the corner watching so she had to always have Renee's brother with her so that he would not try and do anything to her. Meanwhile, she was getting closer and closer to Marcus. Brandon also was noticing that Marcus was always around his wife—and he did not like it one bit—and now he was more determined than ever not to give her a divorce. Oh, he was furious now when he got those divorce papers in the mail. He decided to call up the courthouse and ask for the judge that was presiding over the case and give her a piece of his mind. By the way, that was not a very good idea.

Chante was also depressed over having another child in the custody of her in-laws, but she knew again she had no choice. She had never been on her own and she really didn't know which way to go, but she knew she couldn't go back.

Chapter 23

No Cross, No Crown

Romans 12:17—21, "Recompense to no man for evil. Provide things honest to the sight of all men. If it be possible, as much as lieth in you. Live peaceably with all men. Dearly beloved avenge not yourselves, but rather give place for it is written, "Vengeance is mine," saith the Lord. Therefore, if thine enemy is hungry feed him, give him drink for in so doing they shalt heap coals of fire on his head. Be not overcome of evil, but overcome evil with good."

Even though so many emotions were running through Chante, especially since Brandon was popping up everywhere, she went ranting and raving. The graduation for her GED was coming up soon, divorce procedures were in progress, and she was also developing strong feelings for Marcus. There was a lot going on at one time but most of all, there was a lot of rage; hurt and confusion were the main emotions that seem to be tearing her apart.

Chante knew from going to church that revenge was not good because you should never try to payback somebody with evil. Chante recalled a minister say one time, "It is not for you to avenge yourselves. Put worth in its place and don't let it consume you." Chante knew that she had to get control of her anger. What some people didn't know that saw her was that she had been through a lot of things in her young life, and that there was a lot of anger brewing underneath the surface of that pretty face.

As a person sitting back watching her, I knew that if she didn't get control, it would also consume her. The hurt would take a minute to go away and time does heal all wounds, but she would have to learn patience. She seemed all of a sudden as if life itself had her confused; she really didn't know where to go, and she really didn't know who she could talk to who wouldn't take sides but to just hear her out.

For once in her life, she felt alone and afraid. She felt that there was no one there that really understood the things that she was feeling. She wanted to drop to her knees and ask God to take everything back and make her a child again, but this time in a loving home with loving parents and family. As she looked around, the reality of it was she had no one to depend on but God, and through her prayers and tears she hoped that he would help her make it through.

Chante started thinking that just maybe her grandfather was right about her. Maybe she was a lot like her mother in a negative way. Maybe she would not ever amount to anything, or be important to anyone. Maybe she would turn into an alcoholic or a drug addict with no sense of direction, or perhaps she would meet the same fate as her mother just as her grandfather had pronounced over and over.

It seemed like all of a sudden, everyone around her had an opinion, but no one had a solution. Everyone had advice but no one had the answers to her questions. Everyone wanted to tell her what she should do but no one wanted to accept the truth about why she was in the predicament that she was in.

As far as Marcus and all these new feelings that she was developing for him, she didn't quite understand him or them. Marcus was a man who was used to the ways of the street. Chante had never been around a person like Marcus before. Brandon had been her first, so she was naive to the ways of the world. Chante, since she had started seeing Marcus, started going to clubs and parties and started smoking weed. For she had put church to the side, some of the reason was because of the fun that she started having hanging out with new friends, and some was because every time she went to church, Brandon would be there badmouthing her and calling her names. She felt that everyone was listening to him and had turned their backs on her even though she was not wrong, but that's how he made her feel. She was tired of going to church getting embarrassed or humiliated because Brandon was upset over the divorce, and the fact that he was finally losing control over her.

Sometimes, to get away from the stress of everybody and everything that was going on around her, Chante would walk down to the waterfront and sit by the water and think. A song would sometimes cross her mind. The words were "If you couldn't stand being talked about and if you could not be disappointed sometimes . If you could not stand being lied to and if you think you should always be up and never be down, you had better remember *no cross, no crown.*"

Although Chante had ceased going to church as often as she was going, she knew she needed to get her life together. She knew that she was the only one with the help of God that had to get a grip on her life. She also knew she had to stop being afraid and take control of her own life, and stop depending on someone else to do it for her.

Even I knew that she would have to fight her own battles. I knew that she needed to get back in the church. I also knew that some way, somehow, she had to make a stand.

Chapter 24

FREEDOM AT LAST

Matthew 19:19, "And I say unto you, whosoever shall put away his wife, except it be for fornication, and shall marry another, committeth adultery."

It was a bright sunny Wednesday afternoon when Chante stepped into the courthouse in downtown DC. She had brought along Marcus for moral support, and also because she was scared of Brandon even though they were in a place where there were plenty of policemen. Brandon had made it very adamant that he was not going to sign the divorce decree, and he was never letting her go. He had also said that he was not stepping one foot in the courthouse, and if he didn't show she would not be able to get a divorce from him because he will make sure that she would not be happy with another man, especially Marcus. Brandon even went as far as getting a call to the courthouse to the judge that was presiding over the case, and giving her a piece of his mind although it hurt his case more than it helped it. As a matter of fact, it made it worse.

So when Chante and Marcus got to the courthouse, Marcus decided that it would be better if he waited on the outside of the courthouse rather than on the inside. He knew that nothing would happen to Chante inside the courthouse because she was surrounded by police, but also he didn't want to get Brandon anymore riled up than he already was.

Chante walked into the tiny courtroom feeling very nervous. She had never been in a courtroom before and this room looked different from the courtrooms she had seen on television, and that was because this was one of the smaller courtrooms used for divorce cases.

In the courtroom sat her attorney, the court reporter, and the bailiff. Shortly, in comes Brandon looking like he had not slept in weeks, and it was a good guess that he probably hadn't because he was busy trying to keep his eye on Chante. Plus he had been standing outside of the apartment that Chante was staying at, ranting and raving all night. It didn't bother the tenants because most of them were drunk and didn't pay him any attention. Marcus had decided to stay with her that night just in case there was any trouble. Brandon came in and took his seat at the far end of the table. Then afterward, the judge came in and took her seat. Now it was time to get down to business. The judge asked Chante if she was sure that she wanted to still proceed with the divorce procedures. Chante looked her straight in the eye and said that she did. She also expressed to the judge that there was no reconciliation in the future, and there had been no intimacy encounters between the two since their separation eight months ago.

The judge then turned to Brandon with a scowl on her face, and asked him the same question that she had asked Chante. Brandon replied that he did not want the divorce but if is what Chante wanted then he would comply. He also let the judge know that he was definitely not happy about any of this, but it seemed like he had no choice but to go along with the decision. He also acknowledged that Chante was correct that there had been no intimacy between them since the separation.

After hearing what Brandon had to say, the judge then informed him that she was not happy at the fact that he had called and sent her a nasty message by phone, and that he had proceeded to threaten her in his message. She told him that she had also came to the conclusion whether he had been present or not that this marriage was concluded even before she stepped into the courtroom. She also thanked him for cooperating with the courts because she had been prepared to send a bench warrant out for him.

When Chante walked out of that courtroom, she felt like she had just been given a second chance at life. She felt God had finally heard her cries and prayers, and she was now finally free. *Or was she?*

Outside the courthouse, there was Marcus waiting with a bottle of champagne—it was time to celebrate. If only Chante took the time to go to God's house and celebrate with thanking God for helping her through another milestone than that champagne bottle, she might have been saved from the next set of tears.

In life, we are to learn from our mistakes, but sometimes we put our own selves back in a situation looking for love in the wrong places. We have to learn to make God a part of our lives for he is *a blessing in the storm.*

Proverbs 3:5—7, "Trust in the Lord with all thine heart; and lean not into thine own understanding. In all thy ways acknowledge him, and he shall direct thy paths. Be not wise in thine own eyes; fear the Lord and depart from evil."

In Chante's life, she went through many things in her young life probably more than the average adult. Through her trials and tribulations, she was encouraged to get to know God and to hold on to her faith and trust in him. It seemed that everything in her life was forced upon her but the good thing is there was a blessing in every storm that she went through.

When Chante felt like she wanted to take her life, God showed her he was life and he was always with her. When she made mistakes along the way and people laughed and ridiculed her, God showed her how to grab hold unto him and hold her head up high, and to depend and trust in him.

I am Chante. I was my own best friend because I had none until I found God, and learned to pray and believe that he could make a way out of no way. I had to learn that God is a forgiving God, but it was up to me to make the first step. I cannot say that sometimes it was not scary, but I had to hold on to my faith and God's word.

Today, I am Juanita Witherspoon, no longer hiding behind Chante. For God was my blessing in the storm. *I'm not perfect and I'm still a work in progress, but if it had not been for God then and now, I would not be here to tell this story.*

Sometimes, I wonder if things would have turned out different if I had confided in someone, but then again there was no one that I trusted but God. I regret nothing because experience has been my teacher and guide. I learned that things like insecurities, non-communication, drugs and sex at a young age, do not go together. It just sets you up for trouble.

God put each of us on this earth for a purpose. We are in charge of the choices that we make. Sure, I made plenty of mistakes. I should have stuck to the books and school, but then again I have a lot of 'should-haves.' I can't turn back the hands of time, but I did learn from them and moved on. Of course, I even got angry at myself for getting in some of the situations that I did, and the rage only made me mad with the whole world. But one day, God led me to a mirror to look at myself and then he had me fall to my knees and let go all the pain that was inside, and changed the person that I was because I also was stopping my own blessings from coming.

So on that day he took away all the pain, anger and the low self-esteem. He put a smile on my face. His spirit told me to hold my head high and get back around saints and apostles and members of the church and let him control my life.

I still sometimes have trying days, but when I do, I look to where my strength comes from because with God, there is always a Blessing In The Storm.

About the Author

I am married to a loving and devoted husband. I have three beautiful daughters. I am 57 years old and I thank God every day for what he has brought me through. I am faithful in church. I sing on two choirs and I am on the usher board.

I love reading, writing, traveling, crocheting and coloring. My favorite hobby is being at church giving praises to God, for I would be nothing if it was not for him.

I live in Washington, DC—this is where I was born and raised. My favorite subject in school was English and Reading. I have always wanted a career in writing novels ever since I was in my late twenties, but somehow now felt the courage to do it, and finally, I decided to take a course in writing novels and put my faith in God and just go for it.

I am blessed to have a loving family, friends, and my church family to support me. I am also so proud of myself because when the times got hard and I was ready to give up my dreams of writing, I stayed in the courage to do this not just for myself but to help others.

I do not plan on stopping with this one book. I hope to take you on a journey within my many other stories I have lined up. I thank God for blessing me to be able to write this book for you to enjoy, and I hope along the way I can help someone.